CONTENTS

HOW NOT TO USE A SMARTPHONE

By C.S. Rhymes

INTRODUCTION

I have to say on a personal note, that as a web developer, gadget fanatic and general geek, I have been asked by many of my friends and family to help them out with setting up, using and updating their smartphones (some more than others). This has inspired me to write this book to help out others that are asking common questions about smartphones.

This book is written for all those people that over the years have shied away from getting a smartphone in the past and their old trusty Nokia 3310 has finally beeped its last polyphonic ringtone.

It's designed to give you a head start into the world of smartphones, by helping you understand "How NOT to use a smartphone" so that you can tell your swipe from your pinch and zoom.

BUTTON BASHING

What I have realised is that kids just pick up a smartphone and randomly press buttons (also known as button bashing) until they get the phone to do what they want. Children have no fear when it comes to technology, but adults are very different. This is mainly due to the large investment of several hundreds of pounds (or dollars…) in the smartphone and the last thing they want is to break it.

Smartphone manufacturers spend years developing software for smartphones to make it easy to use and to try and warn you if you are about to do something extremely stupid. Therefore, don't worry too much about pressing a button to find out what it does, just try and think about it logically. At least if it does do something stupid, you have learnt not to do it again…

Try and use your common sense. If the button says delete then it is probably going to delete something. If the button says 'Factory Reset' then this will reset the device to as if it had just come straight out of the factory, so all files and settings will be removed.

OPERATING SYSTEMS

I'll try and make this as painless as possible so please stick with me as you can't really talk about a smartphone without talking about the Operating System (also known as the OS). The OS is the software installed on the phone that runs all of the other applications (or apps).

Lets think about a smartphone as if it were a normal PC. Hopefully you will have heard of Windows. This is the OS on a PC. The PC boots into Windows and has all of the relevant bits (or drivers) to talk to the disc drive, the keyboard, mouse, etc. Once the PC has booted you can then run a program or application, such as a word processor or a game of solitaire. These are separate from the OS but cannot work without the OS to talk between all the input and output devices.

A smartphone is no different. It needs its OS to talk between the input and output devices, the only difference with a phone is that it is all integrated into the one unit. The touch screen acts as the main input device, showing a keyboard on screen when necessary, and your finger acting as the mouse for pointing, clicking and scrolling. Other buttons on the side, such as volume controls and an on/off switch are also examples of input.

The screen is also used as the main output device, showing you messages, web pages and so on. You could also include the speaker as an output device for playing alerts for messages, playing music and ringtones when someone calls you.

There are many different OS's available for smart-phones, but there are currently three main rivals. These are iOS, Android and Windows Phone. These have many similar features but do have significant differences.

IOS

Lets start with iOS. This is available only on smartphones made by Apple, known as iPhones. Apple are
a market leader because they produce premium devices with their own ecosystem. So what do I mean
by ecosystem? You have to use an Apple account
to set up your iPhone and this account is used for
everything, from buying music and apps to backing
up your phone. Apple has a great back up service
built in for your smartphone, called iCloud, that
backs up your contacts, photos, videos and settings
when you are connected to your home wifi. iCloud
is not always enabled by default so try going into
settings and iCloud to check.

Apple also provide a program for your computer
called iTunes that is very easy to use to manage
the content on your phone. If you prefer, you can
back up to your computer, rather than iCloud, using
iTunes.

All of the services from Apple are all really well
integrated and mesh together. The only potential
issue with this is that you are more tied in to buying
additional content, such as music, apps and books
from Apple. There are ways around this, but more

often than not require you to connect your smartphone to your computer to transfer music you have purchased elsewhere on to your smartphone. Apple pioneered their own store to buy this content from and called it the App Store.

If you are willing to commit to Apple for your future purchases then iOS is for you as it is a very polished and easy to use OS. iOS is easy to use as it takes a lot of decision making away from you in terms of settings and controls. Apple encourage you to use the iPhone the way they want you to use it and limit the amount of customisation that is available. Again, this is fine for most users.

ANDROID

Android is made by Google, and like iOS requires an account, but this time its a Google account. Google is trying to link all of its services to its own social network, called Google+, so that you have one identity for all Google sites and services. This works well when integrating with Android as you can use Google+ to automatically back up your photos and video to Google's servers.

In some ways Android is the complete opposite of iOS as rather than limiting what you can change, there is probably a setting for everything you can think off and some you will never even think off, let alone ever see. This means that you are able to completely customise your smartphone and download apps to add additional functionality, such as improved keyboards and "skins".

You are probably asking what on earth is a skin. Well, as well as you being able to customise Android, phone manufacturers and phone networks also customise Android. Google create their base version of Android and then phone manufacturers edit (or "skin" it) with little extra features to make their smartphones stand out from other manufacturers. The networks can then add even more extras, such as their own apps, to the skinned version of Android as well to further differentiate the phone.

This means that two smartphones running the same base version of Android (such as Ice Cream Sandwich, Jelly Bean or Kit Kat (real names!)), but made by two different manufacturers will have very different user interfaces. This gives the consumer (you and me) a large choice between phones and the features available but means that there is often a learning curve when swapping from one manufacturer's version of Android to another.

Anyway, lets look at the Google Android ecosystem. Android has its own store to get games and apps from, like iOS has its App Store, but Android's is called Google Play. The difference with Google Play is that they provide more choice of places to download content from. Google have their own music service (Google Play Music), which you can choose to use, or you have the choice to download an alternative app, such as Amazon Music app, to purchase and download music from.

Choice and freedom is the best way to sum up Android, but you have to try out an Android phone to see if it works for you.

WINDOWS PHONE

Windows Phone is made by Microsoft.

Microsoft have had a mobile operating system for many years, long before iOS and Android existed, but it wasn't particularly amazing. It was called Windows Mobile and when iOS was launched it was blown out of the water and their market share quickly fell. Microsoft came back with Windows Phone, but were a bit late to the party, with the market largely taken up with iOS and Android handsets.

The Windows Phone interface is based on tiles (or squares and rectangles to you and me) that provide information about the app they link to. For example, a tile for a messaging app could display the number of unread messages or a snippet of a received message. The interface is very modern and bright, as well as having nice animations between screens. There are many different manufacturers that use the Windows Phone operating system, with the main manufacturer being Nokia, which has now partnered with Microsoft.

Windows Phone is designed fit alongside the new versions of Windows (8 and 8.1) so if you have used this on your computer and like it then definitely consider getting a Windows Phone.

SUMMARY

These are the main operating systems and hopefully this has given you an understanding of what they can offer. The thing to remember about smartphones and their OS's is that you can't swap from one OS to another. You may get updates and enhancements but you have to stick with the OS for the life of the phone.

APPS

Previously we have learnt about operating systems (OS), the software which makes the smartphone work. Now we are talking about Apps. Apps, short for applications, are the programs that run on a smartphone.

PRE INSTALLED APPS

Some apps come pre installed on your smartphone for the core functionality, such as the caller app (to make phone calls), the contacts app, the text messaging app and the web browser. Other common pre installed apps include email, calendar, music player and camera.

Although these apps are fairly common, the functionality can vary widely between different smartphones, from the OS, the version of the OS and the manufacturer of the handset. These apps can also receive updates along with the OS but they can also be updated separately, adding new features and functionality to the apps.

Chances are, you never updated the software on your old mobile phone and the software stayed the same from the day you bought it, but smartphones and their software is advancing all the time. To help keep smartphones more consistent, regular updates are released. App updates are released through the devices app store.

WHAT IS AN APP STORE?

Put simply, an app store is a place you buy and download apps from on your smartphone. Some apps are free and some you have to pay for, whereas others are free to download, but then you can purchase items from within the app.

Apple created the first widely used app store to go alongside their iPhone, allowing iPhone owners to download new games, new functionality and new digital content, such as music and films, on their smartphone. Android and Windows Phone also have their own app stores.

When smartphones were first released, there were not many smartphone optimised websites, so companies made free apps instead so that smartphone users can use their services when out and about. Other people realised that they could make money out of app stores by developing and selling their own games. These two factors led to a boom in the development and downloading of apps.

The app store is where you can get new apps for

your smartphone and where you can download updates to your existing apps. Each app has a version number, allowing your smartphone to identify if there are any updates available. Updates can be as simple as bugfixes to whole new versions of apps.

THINGS TO CONSIDER WHEN DOWNLOADING APPS

The first thing to consider when downloading an app is whether you have to pay for it or not. It is very easy to download lots of apps at 99p each without realising how much money you have spent overall. Obviously, it's up to you how much you want to spend, this is just a bit of advice to keep track of what you have bought.

You may also want to consider if you need to make in app purchases. Some apps require you to purchase additional content within the app to unlock additional features or extra lives in the app. You should also be aware if the app requires a subscription and not just a one off payment. An example of this is a magazine app that may let you purchase one off copies or you may subscribe to the magazine to automatically get the next edition and the payment will be taken directly from your account.

Free apps may have adverts within them that can potentially interrupt gameplay. You may be able to make an in app purchase to remove the adverts.

When you buy an app you need to download and install it to your smartphone to use it. Consider the size of the download before you commit to downloading the app, especially considering if it is best to connect to wifi before starting the download. Some phone contracts have a limited amount of data you can download each month. If this is the case for you then try and connect to wifi before downloading large apps to avoid additional data charges.

We'll discuss storage in a bit more detail later, but lets just say smartphones have a finite amount of memory and you want to consider the storage requirements of an app before downloading. If you don't have enough memory available then you may need to delete some existing apps.

APP REVIEWS AND RATINGS

The app store allows you view other users ratings and reviews, as well as make your own rating and write your own review of an app. These ratings allow you to get an impression of what others think of an app before you choose to buy it. Users that are particularly unhappy with an app will rate an app 1 star. This is the lowest score available as you can't rate an app with zero stars.

The highest rating is 5 stars, but its worth reading the most recent reviews before buying an app based on its average rating. The most recent reviews will tell you if there are problems with the latest version of the app. For example, the first version of the app may have many 5 star reviews, but the latest update (version 2) may crash a lot, so users that have updated will post their unhappy feedback with a review. The average feedback may still be high as the rating is based on all versions of the app.

If you want to leave your own review then its worth going into a bit of detail about what you especially enjoyed or disliked about the app. App developers enjoy getting positive feedback but they always want to fix any issues that you may find to try and make their app the best app available. This is especially important for negative feedback as its very difficult to replicate the issues you may have experienced without detail of what you were doing when the issue occurred.

If an update has been released that resolves your issue, then why not update your review to reflect this as well? The developer will appreciate it and so will other users of the app store.

MOVING APPS

There are some apps on Android that allow you to move them to an external memory card within the phone and free up some of the phones memory. This is on an app by app basis so sometimes there is no choice but to delete the app to free up space.

DELETING APPS

You don't have to keep an app forever, even if you have bought it, it can be deleted to make space for new apps. The easiest way of removing or deleting an app from your smartphone is to go to the app store and find the app you want to remove. There is normally an option within the app in the app store to let you remove the app from your device.

App stores remember that you have purchased an app so if you delete it (either on purpose or by mistake) then you can re download it to your device from the app store. Although you can delete and download the app again without paying for it, your progress may not be saved and you might have to start the app from scratch.

Certain apps cannot be deleted, either because they are essential to the operation of your smartphone, such as the camera or dialer app, or because the manufacturer or phone network operator has decided they don't want you to download it. Personally I find not being able to delete some of the pre-installed apps quite annoying as they are taking up memory that could be used for something else.

ROTATING YOUR SMARTPHONE

To make the most of the screen space available on a smartphone, you can rotate it to change your phone from Portrait to Landscape mode. The smartphone has built in sensors to detect which orientation (portrait or landscape) is being used. When you are on your home screen (without any apps open and you can see the app icons) the phone is normally in portrait mode.

When you launch an app you normally have the option to rotate your smartphone to choose how you want it laid out. If you are sending a text message or an email you can rotate your phone into landscape mode to use a larger keyboard. You may also want to use landscape mode if you are watching a video.

Some apps are fixed to have only one orientation. For these you have no choice as to how it is displayed. Apps that are fixed orientation are normally created that way as it would be unusable the other way round.

COMMON TOUCHSCREEN CONTROLS

As discussed earlier, the main way to interact with your smartphone is to use the touchscreen. If you haven't used a touchscreen before then this may be one of the largest initial learning curves for you, but once you learn the basics you will see that the majority of apps make use of the same actions for consistency.

Actions on a touchscreen? What are you on about? Well, lets go back to the computer analogy again. With a keyboard on your computer you can press one letter key at a time to input text, but you can also press and hold shift and then press a letter to get a capital letter. Using a mouse you can click or double click to perform an action, such as opening a folder, but you can also click and drag to move a file into a folder.

Rather than making a touchscreen as simple as one click at a time, it also allows movements and multiple touches at the same time to perform different action.

Just one other thing to mention from helping my friends and family is that a smartphone touch-screen is very sensitive. By this I mean you don't have to jab the screen with your finger as hard as you can to get it to work, simply tap the screen gently.

Anyway, back on to the touchscreen controls and actions. Have you heard of swipe or pinch and zoom?

TAP

This is the most basic control for touchscreen and I'm pretty sure you can figure this one out, but thought I had better include it to be thorough. This simply involves tapping the screen with a finger. An example of this is tapping an app icon to launch the app, or pressing a contact telephone number to call someone.

SWIPING

Swiping is when you quickly swipe across the screen with your finger, in any direction, and then move your finger off the screen. For example, you can swipe up, down, left or right. Apps such as image galleries use swipe to navigate between images in the gallery.

Swiping from the top or bottom of the screen
Depending on your smartphone model, you can also swipe a menu down from the top of the screen, or up from the bottom of the screen. Swiping down from the top of the screen normally displays your notifications. These are items such as missed calls, messages and emails.

Swiping up from the bottom of the screen is used on iOS 7 to display a settings menu to turn things on and off, such as wifi and bluetooth.

DRAG AND DROP

This is similar to a mouse and computer where you click on something to select it and, whilst still holding the mouse button, move it somewhere else. You can also do this on a smartphone, but sometimes you have to press and hold the item you want to move for a second or two to select it, before dragging it to where you want it to go. An example of this is dragging an app icon from one screen to another or moving an app icon on top of another to create a folder.

PINCH AND ZOOM

When smartphones were first launched, there were not many mobile friendly websites. Therefore, you had a website load up on your 3.5 inch smartphone screen that was designed for a standard 15 inch display. Obviously, this led to the text being ridiculously small. To get around this, you can zoom into the page to read part at a time.

You can zoom into the web page by using pinch and zoom, basically pinching your fingers together, placing them both on the screen and then moving them apart. The further apart you move your fingers, the more you zoom in. You can also reverse the action (moving your fingers closer together) to zoom out of the page.

This action is now widely used across many different apps, such as maps, where you want to be able to zoom in to see more detail of the map, or zoom out to see an overview of the area.

DOUBLE TAP TO ZOOM

As well as being able to pinch and zoom into webpages, you can double tap to zoom. Webpages are made out of different elements, such as a paragraph of text or an image. Double tapping on one of these elements automatically zooms the view in to fit the element to the width of the screen. For example, you are viewing a webpage with an image that is half the width of the webpage, double tapping on the image would zoom the view in to fit the half of the page with the image in.

CONTACTS AND LINKING ACCOUNTS

Believe it or not, you can make calls with a smartphone! The phone part of smartphone kind of gives that away, but with all the other technology available, such as text messaging, emails and social networks you may prefer a different communication method to calling someone.

Anyway, to call someone you can use the phone app. You can do like you did on your old home phone and dial a number into the keypad each time you want to call it, but there is a much better way than this. Smartphones have the ability to store contacts.

CONTACTS

With your old phone, you may of had to store your phone numbers on the sim card. With a smartphone there is much more storage on the phone, allowing you to store your contacts on your phone. This also means that you can store a lot more information, rather than just name and number, such as an email address, home and mobile number, address, website, and more. You can even assign a photo to your contacts to help you recognise or remember them.

If we go back to the different operating systems again, they offer ways of storing your contacts online, as well as on your smartphone. This allows you to backup all of your contacts so that you can login to another device and retrieve all of your contacts. Gone are the days of having to manually enter hundreds of contacts from one phone to another.

Apple automatically backs up your contacts using its iCloud service. You can even view your contacts online from any device using icloud.com and signing in with your apple account.

Google also offers a similar service for its Android operating system but it may not be enabled by default, depending on your smartphone model. Again, you can view your contacts online, this time using contacts.google.com and logging in with your Google account.

Windows Phone also offers a contacts backup service. You just need to log in to the device with your microsoft account (such as hotmail, msn or outlook.com).

MANAGING MULTIPLE ACCOUNTS

As well as using the single default account, you can normally combine your contacts from different accounts on your smartphone. An example of this is that you have an iPhone but use Google to manage your contacts. You can sign in to both your Apple account and Google account on your iPhone and have access to both contacts on your device.

This, however, doesn't mean that the the accounts are merged. The accounts remain separate but you can view them side by side.

It is recommended to try and pick one service that you would like to use and stick with it, rather than having multiple fragmented contact lists. This makes it easier if you have a smartphone and a tablet, ensuring all your contacts are synced between them.

Using two different accounts could be preferred by

some, for example, by people who want to keep their work and private contacts separate. You could store all of your work contacts with a Microsoft account and your private contacts with your Google account.

SOCIAL ACCOUNTS

You may also have a lot of contacts from social media sites, such as Facebook and Twitter. Some smartphones allow you to combine your social contacts with your normal phone contacts and get their latest social updates alongside their phone number. Other smartphones deliberately try and avoid this from happening.

I find that it can become confusing trying to identify which contacts have phone numbers and which don't. This can also lead to contacts being duplicated in your contacts list and you have to manually combine the contacts together. Personally, I like to keep social contacts separate from my phone contacts. This way I know I have phone numbers for all my phone contacts and that I am not sending them a public message by using social media by mistake.

This may sound a bit silly, but it can be very easy to send someone a tweet (through twitter) rather than a normal text message on some devices as the contacts and services become so closely combined. I'm sure that you have sent your friends a message that you would rather stay private and not published on the internet.

MESSAGING

You can send and receive a wide variety of messages using your smartphone, including text messages, Multimedia Messages (MMS), email and instant messages.

TEXT MESSAGES

The standard way of sending messages is to use SMS (Short Message Service) or text messages. These are simple, text only messages and allow up to 160 characters per message, although most smartphones will join longer messages together so they appear as one message.

Text messaging is one of the standard pre installed apps, but for Android, there are other apps that can be downloaded that can also manage your text messages. An example of this is Google+ Hangouts, which is also used to send messages to your friends using Google Plus. Apple use iMessage to manage your text messages and provides additional features when sending messages to other iPhone users, such as telling you when someone has read your message and allows users to send and receive messages on other Apple devices, such as iPads and Mac computers.

Many contracts include a certain amount of text messages per month, whereas others may charge per message. This charge is why people move to using instant messages instead as these are sent through the internet, rather than using your phone allocation.

MULTIMEDIA MESSAGES

Multimedia messages allow you to send additional media, such as pictures, sound and even video to other smartphone users. The downside to multimedia messages is that they are not normally included in phone contracts and that they can cost more to send than text messages. Also, people with older phones may not be able to receive them, instead they will be sent a link to download the image, sound or video from.

They are still limited to the size that can be sent and received, like text messages, so the pictures and sounds are normally compressed to fit this size limit. Videos also need to be quite short and low quality to be sent.

If you want to send a high quality picture or video then why not try using email instead.

EMAIL

Using email on your phone is great way to send larger, high resolution photos to others. Sending emails will use your data allowance so if you don't have a lot of internet allowance each month try connecting to your wifi before sending.

There is a standard email app in most smartphones but there are also specific email apps for certain email services. Examples of this include Outlook.com (for Windows email accounts) and Gmail (for Google Gmail accounts). Downloading the apps may provide additional features that are not available on the standard email app, such as being able to search older emails that are not on your device. Check out the reviews and if you prefer, you can always revert to the standard email app.

One issue with having email on your phone is that it constantly checks for new messages and it will notify you of new emails whatever the time of day. As you can imagine, its a bit annoying getting email notifications in the middle of the night and waking you up. Some apps have a quiet time setting that allows you to turn off notifications between certain times. The other issue with email apps constantly checking for new email is that it can use up your battery and your data allowance. To avoid this, try changing your apps settings from push (constantly checking) to every 15 minutes or every 30 minutes. Emails are normally less time sensitive than text messages so checking less often is less of a worry.

INSTANT MESSAGING

Rather than sending text messages, you can use different apps to send instant messages. Instant messaging is more like having an online chat and normally allows you to send smiley faces to each other (known as emoticons or emojis). Instant messaging uses your data connection (internet), rather than your message allowance. Again, if at home, why not connect to your wifi if you don't have a large data allowance on your contract.

There are many instant messaging apps available, with some of the most popular being Facebook Messenger, Google Hangouts and Skype. To use these apps you have to have an existing account or set up a new account. Facebook messenger is good as it allows you to send messages to all of your friends on Facebook, whether they have the Messenger app installed or not. Google hangouts uses your Google Plus contacts and Skype is now owned by Microsoft so it can use your Microsoft contacts.

CAMERAS

The majority of smartphones have a camera and most have two. The camera on the rear is normally the best of the two and is the primary camera for taking pictures and videos. The camera on the front is normally lower quality and is used as a webcam for making video calls and for using with apps such as Skype.

The camera quality and available settings vary widely between different smartphones but there are some common features that are available on most devices. These include swapping the camera to use the front facing camera, panorama and recording video.

WHAT IS A SELFIE?

You may have heard of the term "Selfie". This is when you take a picture of yourself using the front facing camera on your phone. To do this you need to press the button to swap the camera to use the front facing camera rather than the rear facing camera by default.

PANORAMA

A panorama is when you take a series of photos that are then stitched together to make one large photo. Panoramas are great for wide landscape pictures as they can capture much more than a normal picture. Panoramas are best when there is not a lot of movement as the movement can cause glitches in the final image when they are stitched together.

RECORDING VIDEO

You can also record video with your smartphone. The quality of video can vary between smartphones but many record in full high definition (HD), some record in 4k (four times HD). The thing to remember with recording video is that it takes up much more memory than pictures.

When recording a video, try and keep the smartphone as steady as possible as it is easy to wobble the camera, which in turn can make the video difficult to watch later. Another thing to consider is light levels. Try and make sure there is enough light when recording a video as the flash doesn't normally come on when recording a video.

LOOKING AFTER YOUR SMARTPHONE

You've paid a few hundred pounds for your new smartphone so you probably want to look after it. I have lost count of the number of iPhones I have seen over the years with cracked screens. Although new smartphones are built extremely well, out of robust materials, there is always a chance of scratching or even cracking the case or the screen. So how can you protect your smartphone?

SCREEN PROTECTORS

To help prevent you scratching your screen you can buy a plastic screen protector. Sounds obvious really. You can buy a really cheap screen protector from the market or a site like Ebay, just make sure that it is designed for your exact phone model and check the sellers reviews (if using Ebay) to see if there are any complaints about the fit. I would advise against buying a screen protector that you cut down to fit as it won't fit as well and the edges will probably catch and the screen protector will come loose. Screen protectors are not sticky, they simply use static to stick to the screen.

Before fitting your screen protector, ensure that the screen is free from dust and grease as this will become trapped under the screen protector and will look like a small bubble. The best time to fit the protector is straight after getting your smartphone out of the box to ensure there is as little chance of dust and fingerprints getting on the screen as possible.

CASE

There are many cases you can buy to fit your smartphone. From personal experience I would recommend buying a case from the same manufacturer as your smartphone. This is because you can guarantee that it will fit and that it will fit well.

Try not to get a case where the cover over the screen cannot be tucked out of the way when you are using the phone (actually as a phone). Why is this? I just find it so amusing when people are on the phone and their case is flapping about in the wind and hitting them in the face. Maybe this is just me?

INSURANCE

Insurance is a tricky subject to cover. As stated previously if you drop your phone you can scratch or even crack the screen, even with a case and screen protector. So should you get insurance out on your phone? I'm afraid this one is up to you.

All I can advise is to consider how much your phone costs from new and to check how much second hand models go for on sites like ebay. Compare this cost against the overall cost of insurance to see what is cheaper as you may be better off saving the money each month and pay for a new smartphone if you do ever break it.

The other option is to ask if you are able to send your phone back to the manufacturer for repairs and how much it generally costs. Just remember that it may take a couple of months to be sent away and come back and be repaired (and you could be without a phone in the mean time).

Another option is to check whether you get any mobile phone insurance with your bank. I recently discovered that it had been included for years, but that I had to register my phone with the service to activate the insurance. Make sure you read the small print as free insurance may not cover the full cost, or only up to a certain cost.

PIN & SECURITY

If you have the option to lock your smartphone with a PIN then I would recommend it. For convenience, smartphone apps stay signed in so if someone took your phone then they could have access to various email and social accounts, as well as making phone calls and potentially buying items with your account (although most require you to sign in for each purchase). Mobile banking apps should request that you login each time you use it, if they don't, uninstall it and don't use it.

UPDATING SOFTWARE

One thing that may get overlooked by smartphone users is updating the smartphones software. This is really important to do as it loads in the latest features available, but also provides bug fixes and security updates. You may have to update older smartphones by plugging them into the computer, but new smartphones download the update files themselves and then ask you to install it.

Before completing an update, make sure that you have backed up and content that is important to you, such as contacts, photos and videos. This is a useful precaution if the update doesn't work as intended. This is less common but can still happen on the odd occasion. Also, make sure the battery is charged and that you follow the instructions and when it says please wait, you wait and don't start pressing buttons or trying to turn it on and off as this can corrupt the update process.

If an update doesn't work as expected, then either take the smartphone back to where you bought it from and see if they can restore it, or go to the manufacturers website for advice. Most manufacturers provide software to download that can be used to try and restore your phone to a previous state. Again, make sure you read the instructions carefully and follow them to the letter.

SUMMARY

Hopefully this book has given you a good introduction into smartphones and their day to day operation. Remember, don't be scared, try to think what a kid would do and feel free to press buttons to discover what they do, but use your common sense.

If you find an app difficult to use then let the app developer know by leaving a review on the app store so that they can make it better. Just like app developers, I am always looking for feedback. Why not leave a comment on the Amazon kindle store or alternatively, send me a tweet on twitter using @chrisrhymes and let me know what you think or if there are any additional topics you would like information on.